Desert Island Stitches:™
Take–Along Idea Books
for Painted Canvas Embellishment

By Carole H. Lake &
Michael E. Boren

Stitches Plain and Fancy®
© 2015 StitchPlay Designs®

4003 Edgefield Ct., Austin, TX 78731
(512) 349-0390 FAX (512) 628-3560
carole@stitchplay.com
michael@stitchplay.com

Acknowledgments:

Thanks to our friends who nit-picked, commented and were the best cheerleaders ever:

Kathy Gordon
Jessica Tew
Margaret Johnson
Evelyn Petschek
Evie Faichney

For production help and boundless creativity:

Sue Dulle
Sherrie Zimmerman

For endless patience and meticulous work:

Sir Speedy Printing and Marketing #4092
3818 Far West Blvd.
Austin, TX 78731

To our students, past and present, who have made comments and suggestions which have made this material infinitely better. You know who you are!

And, finally to David and Larry, who knew we were lying when we told them we were never going to write another book!

Michael and Carole

Welcome to *Desert Island Stitches*, a series of take-along books for painted canvas embellishment.

The inspiration for this series of books and its title has a most unlikely origin. It is from a radio show long heard on the BBC, entitled "Desert Island Discs." The idea for the show was to invite several musicians and other notables to identify those discs of recorded music that they would choose to take to a virtual desert island, if they could only take a very few.

Instead of discs, we wondered which stitch books you would take if you were cast away on a desert island?

In this series of books, we will help you pack your stitching bag for that trip. That island might, in fact, be one you visit on vacation, or it may be a frame of mind when you enter into your usual stitching station.

The books in this series will provide you with ideas for the different spaces that you are likely to encounter on a painted canvas. This first volume presents ideas for the smallest of spaces.

We have included classic stitches, as well as many, many variations and innovations.

The book is light and easy to carry, but it contains what you will need, and hopefully enjoy, while you are stitching in that desert island paradise, be it near to home or far away. We even put in some of our favorite stitching tips in each section!

We hope that your trip will be enjoyable, rewarding, and lead to productive new stitching adventures.

Carole and Michael
StitchPlay Designs

This is not your usual stitch book. This is an idea book. Reach for this book when you don't know what you want to put in a particular space!

Here are some ideas to help you get the most out of the book.

• The Stitches

You will find some of the basic stitches for needlepoint in this book, plus many additional patterns that can be created with them. We start with the most basic stitch of all, the tent stitch, and then move on through diagonal, oblique, straight and cross stitches.

All of the stitches and patterns in this volume were selected as particularly suitable for small spaces. They can be worked in an area that is less than a square inch in size. It is always important that your stitches be in proportion to the size of the area on the canvas.

Remember that one square inch on 18-count canvas is only 18-threads by 18-threads square. The stitch diagrams and patterns in this book may look large, but that is because the book uses a large grid so that it will be easy to read. Most of the patterns here are less than 12-threads by 12-threads, so they will fit in the smallest of spaces. Of course, that doesn't mean you cannot use them in a larger space (with more repeats!).

• The Diagrams:

On the first page of almost every section, you will find a diagram of the basic stitch in dark black ovals, with numbering. This is the starting point from which the patterns are created.

Most of the patterns are shown in combinations of white ovals and black ovals. The shading serves to help define the stitch pattern visually, plus it suggests possible pattern changes to you. You can do all of these stitches in solid colors, but you can also work them in multiple threads and/or colors.

• The Patterns:

A variety of patterns, based on the basic stitch unit, are presented. You can make even more patterns yourself!

Some of the patterns are presented vertically and some are presented horizontally. Remember that you can always easily visualize a different orientation by simply rotating the book! Many of the patterns can also be worked in mirror-image, changing the slant of the stitch to go in the opposite direction. If you can't figure out what a stitch would look like mirror-imaged, place the diagram page on the surface of a window, and you'll see the mirror image when you look through the back of the page.

Sometimes a pattern will show an open or 'unstitched' space. You can fill those spaces with beads, cross stitches, or tent stitches. However, the best idea many times is to just leave the space open and let the beautiful paint on the canvas show through. This is a clever way to show shading, and to enhance your painted canvas.

• **Numbering:**
Very few of the patterns in this book are numbered. That is because there is almost never one set, perfect, correct way in which a stitch pattern must be worked.

The needlepoint police are not watching!

When you start to stitch an area of the canvas, the first thing you should do is to decide where to start the stitch. This really depends on the shape of the space you are stitching. We often like to start with a row of the stitch going across the widest part of the area. This sets the pattern. You then fill in the pattern outward to the edges of the space.

If you can't decide where to start, the default is to start in the upper right or upper left corner of the area.

• How to Find a Stitch:

The book is divided into 5 sections: Tent Stitches, Diagonal Stitches, Oblique Stitches, Straight Stitches and Cross Stitches. These sections are divided within the book by blue pages.

The tent stitches are the smallest, and many times are the default choice for the tiniest areas. Diagonal and oblique stitches are favorites because they fit nicely and compensate well. Straight stitches are used to create a vertical or horizontal look, while cross stitches are often used for texture.

We think the best way to locate a stitch that suits the space you want to stitch is simply to flip through the book, first forwards, and then from the back. Then, turn the book upside down, and do it again. Make a note of stitches that:

> (a) look interesting,
> (b) look like they will be in proportion to the space you are stitching, and
> (c) in which the pattern of the stitch runs in an appropriate direction for what you are stitching.

Enjoy!

Tent stitches are a single stitch over one canvas intersection, worked from lower left to upper right. They are the smallest of possible needlepoint stitches, so, of course, that's where we start for the smallest of spaces!

Tent stitch can be worked in one of two patterns. These are:
• **Basketweave** (sometimes called diagonal tent because it is worked diagonally across the canvas). This is the sturdiest stitch, and requires attention to the grain of the canvas. The back of this stitch, when worked correctly, looks like a woven basket, thus, the name.

• **Continental stitch** is worked in rows, usually for outlines or for small areas where there isn't room for the pattern of basketweave. When worked correctly, the carriage of thread on the back of the canvas creates a firm padding.
Note: If you only see a tiny bit of thread on the back, you are doing 'half-cross stitch', and that is never correct because it distorts the weave of the canvas.

Patterns of tent stitches are created by leaving spaces between the stitches, by changing colors, by reversing the direction of the tent stitch or by changing threads. Some of these stitch patterns have commonly used names, and others are patterns created to suit the area you are stitching. Often changing the stitch sequence of a pattern changes the way it looks on the surface.

When you are stitching a very small space, always consider using tent stitch or a variation of tent stitch first.

Basketweave!

Working the basketweave stitch correctly (with the grain of the canvas) is a key ingredient for making your work smooth and consistent. Basketweave is worked diagonally across the canvas, paying special attention to the weave of the canvas. Each canvas intersection's top thread is either vertical or horizontal.

Take your first stitch in the upper right corner of an area, and then look at the canvas intersection just to the left of this stitch. If a vertical thread is on top of that intersection, place your second stitch over that intersection as the start of a diagonal-down row. If a horizontal thread is on top of that intersection, place your second stitch over the intersection immediately below the first stitch, to begin a diagonal-up row.

Having trouble remembering? We use the 'firehouse method': always go up the ladder (up over the horizontal intersections) and down the pole (down over the vertical intersection).

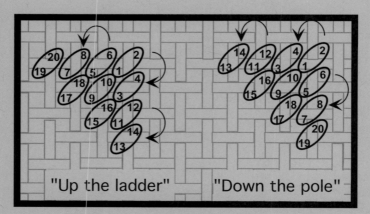

"Up the ladder"   "Down the pole"

Remember: never stitch two rows going in the same direction next to each other; and, end your thread by running under the stitches either horizontally or vertically - never diagonally.

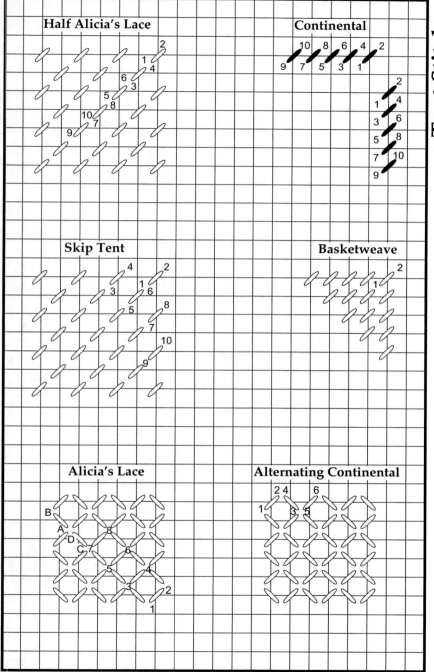

Half Alicia's Lace

Continental

Skip Tent

Basketweave

Alicia's Lace

Alternating Continental

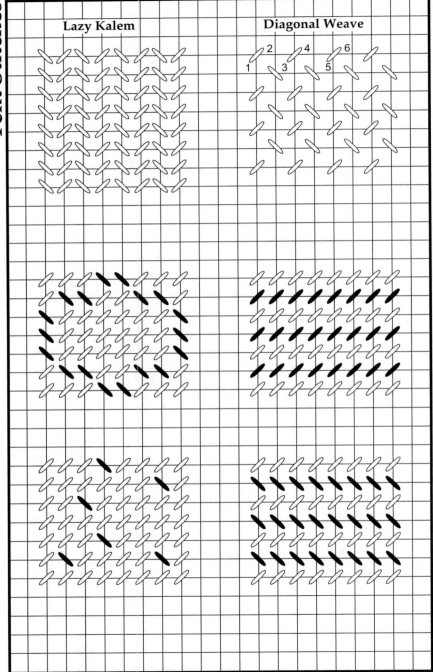

Tent Stitches

Lazy Kalem

Diagonal Weave

Diagonal stitches are stitches that are worked across the canvas at a 45° angle. The tent stitch is, of course, the smallest diagonal stitch, worked over only one intersection. In this section of the book, we branch out to longer stitches. Because we are considering small spaces, most of the stitches in this book will be over combinations of 1, 2, 3 and 4 intersections.

The standard versions of these stitches are worked from lower left to upper right, but never forget that you can reverse the direction. A handy way to visualize this is to simply turn your book a quarter turn! You will see that we present many of the stitches in their rotated form.

We will start with three basic units of diagonal stitches and the patterns created from them. The mosaic stitch is a 1-2-1 pattern, which is a combination of a stitch over-1, a stitch over-2 and a stitch over-1. The cashmere stitch follows a 1-2-2-1 pattern, and the Scotch stitch is made up of a 1-2-3-2-1 sequence. From there we will move into a variety of diagonal variations and patterns, all of which fit into small areas.

All of these stitch patterns can be worked as a solid unit using a single thread. Many times in a very small area, that's the best idea. However, you can make interesting variations by using multiple threads, using multiple colors, reversing some of the stitches, changing directions and more! We have created some of these possibilities for you by shading some of the stitches within the patterns.

How Much Thread Should You Buy?

There's no one right answer to this question. The thread market is ever changing. Companies come and companies go. The one constant is that differing dyelots are a nightmare if you run out of thread partway through a project. Our theory is that you can never have too much thread. Never buy 'just enough'. It is far better to have way too much than to be 10" short.

A rule of thumb is that 1 square inch of basketweave stitch on 18-count canvas uses about 1.5 yards of thread. Even if you are not doing basketweave, this gives you a nice average amount of thread to buy. We always round up to 2 yards, just in case, anyway!

Start by roughly measuring an area on your canvas and multiply by 2 yards. *Use the size of your thumbprint for approximately 1 square inch or your palm for approximate 4 square inches.* Let's say the sail on your sailboat is about 2" x 3" = 6 square inches. So, theoretically, you will need about 12 yards of thread. If you are buying 10-yard skeins, you are probably okay with 2 skeins. However, if your sail is 3" x 3" = 9 square inches, that is about 18 yards, and we'd highly recommend buying a third skein. Be sure you get the same dyelot. Have your shop order what you will need in the same dyelot, rather than take a chance on running out.

Take into account your personal stitching style, as well. Carole always uses about 20% more thread than Michael does on the same project. (She blames it on the cat!) If you are a frugal stitcher, you can buy less, but if you know you tend to run out, be sure to buy extra. If you tend to rip out a lot, buy extra. It is never a waste of money to buy too much thread.

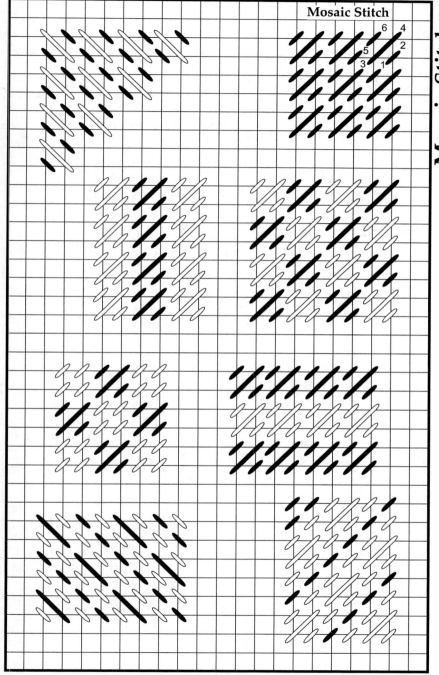

Mosaic Stitch

Mosaic Stitches

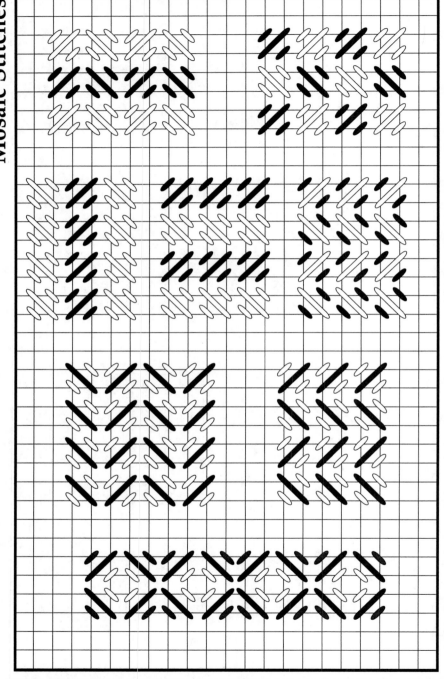

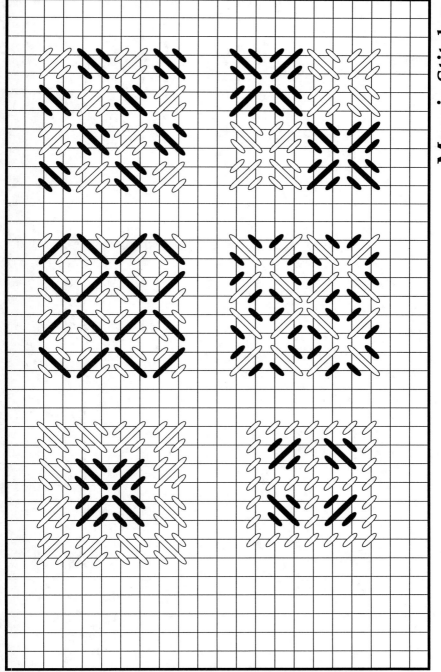

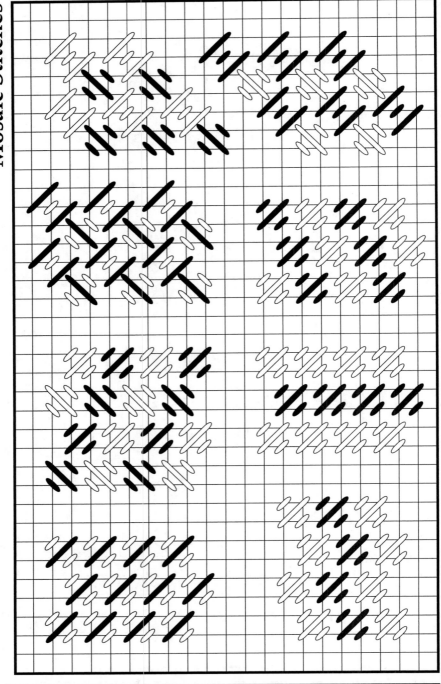

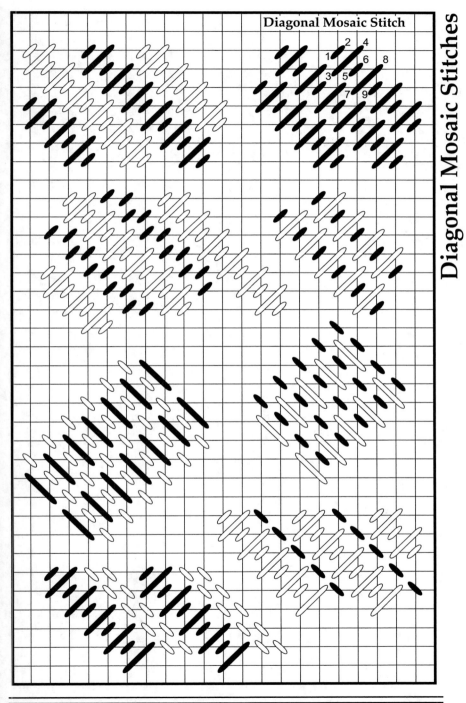

Diagonal Mosaic Stitch

Cashmere Stitch

2 4
1 6
3 8
5 7

Cashmere Stitches

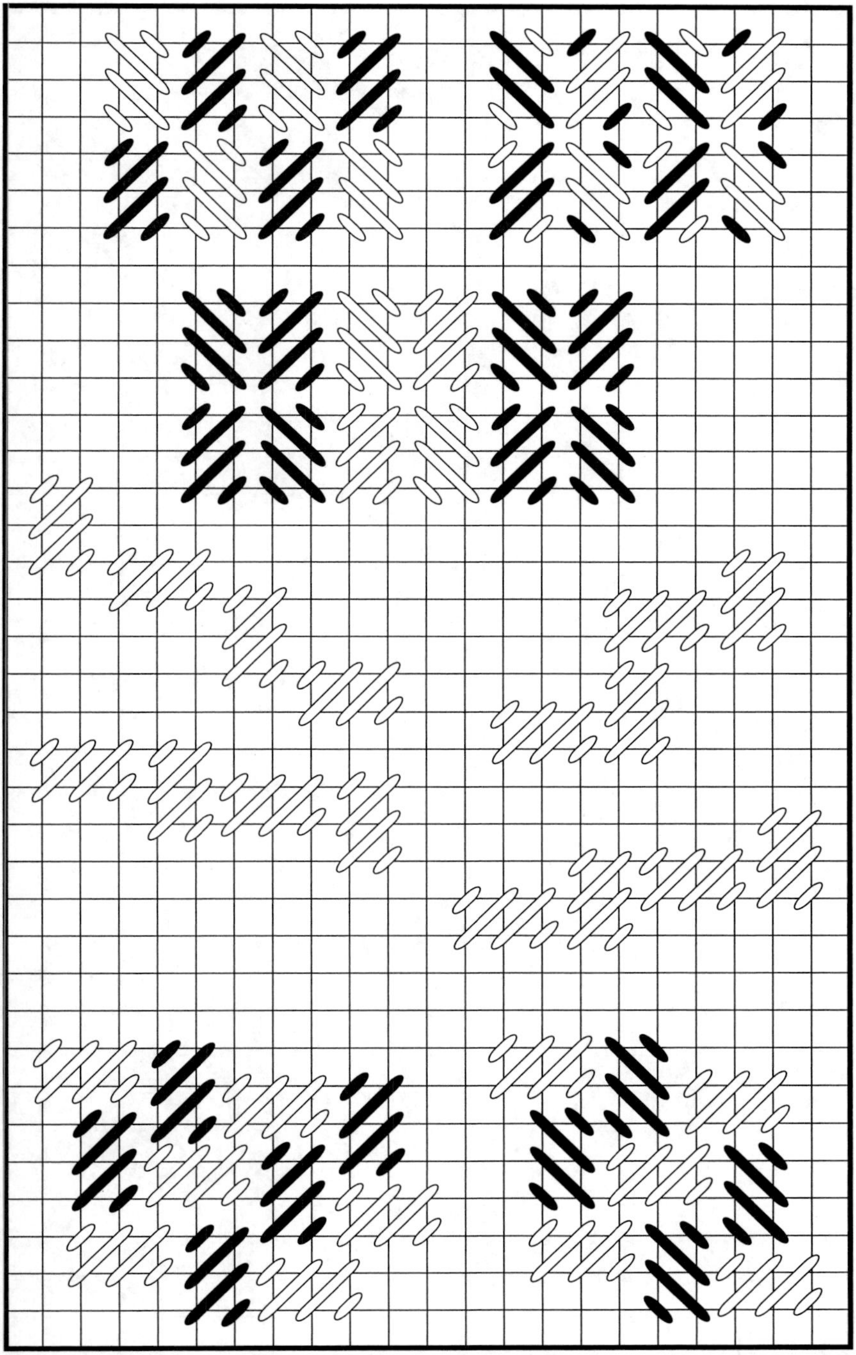

Cashmere Stitches

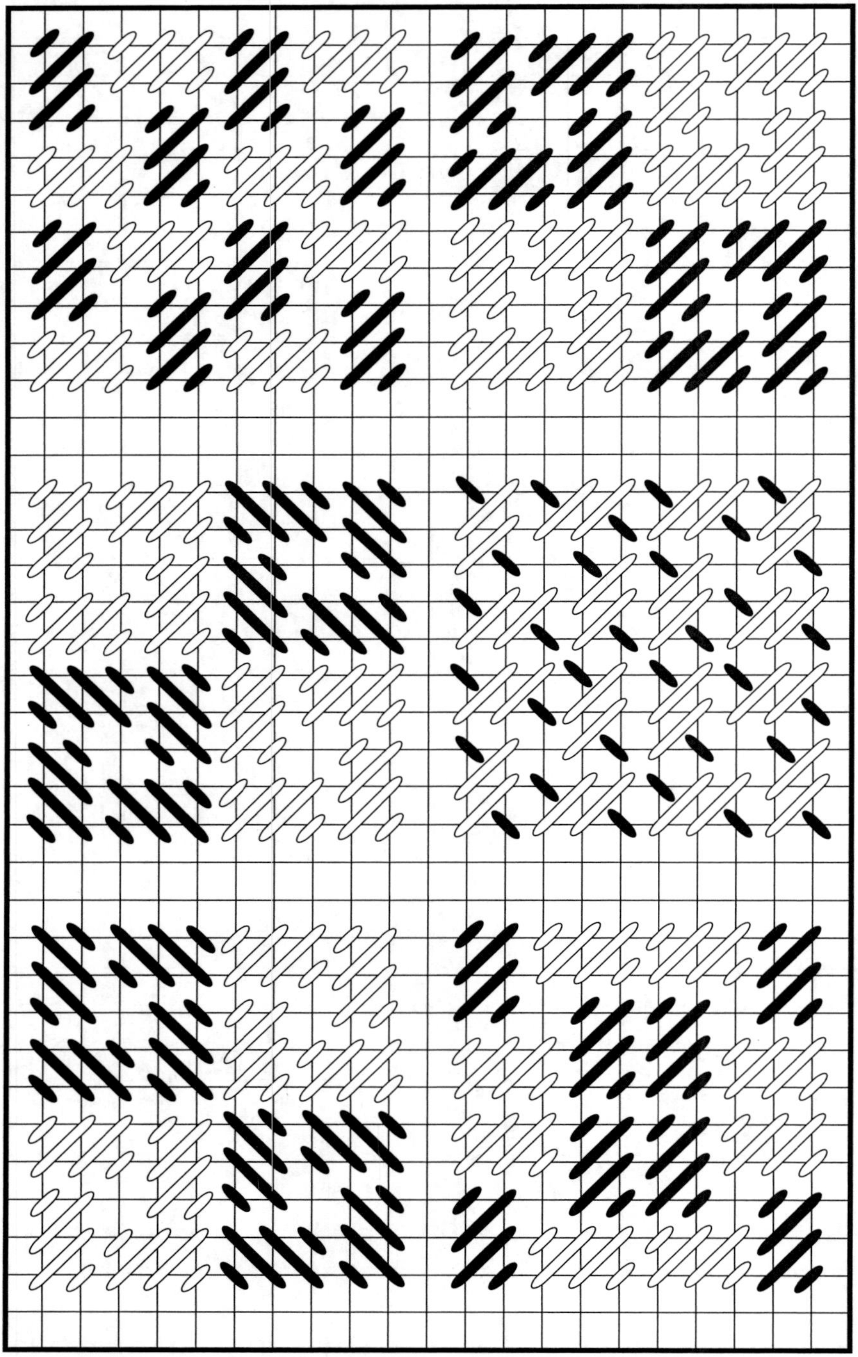

Cashmere Stitches

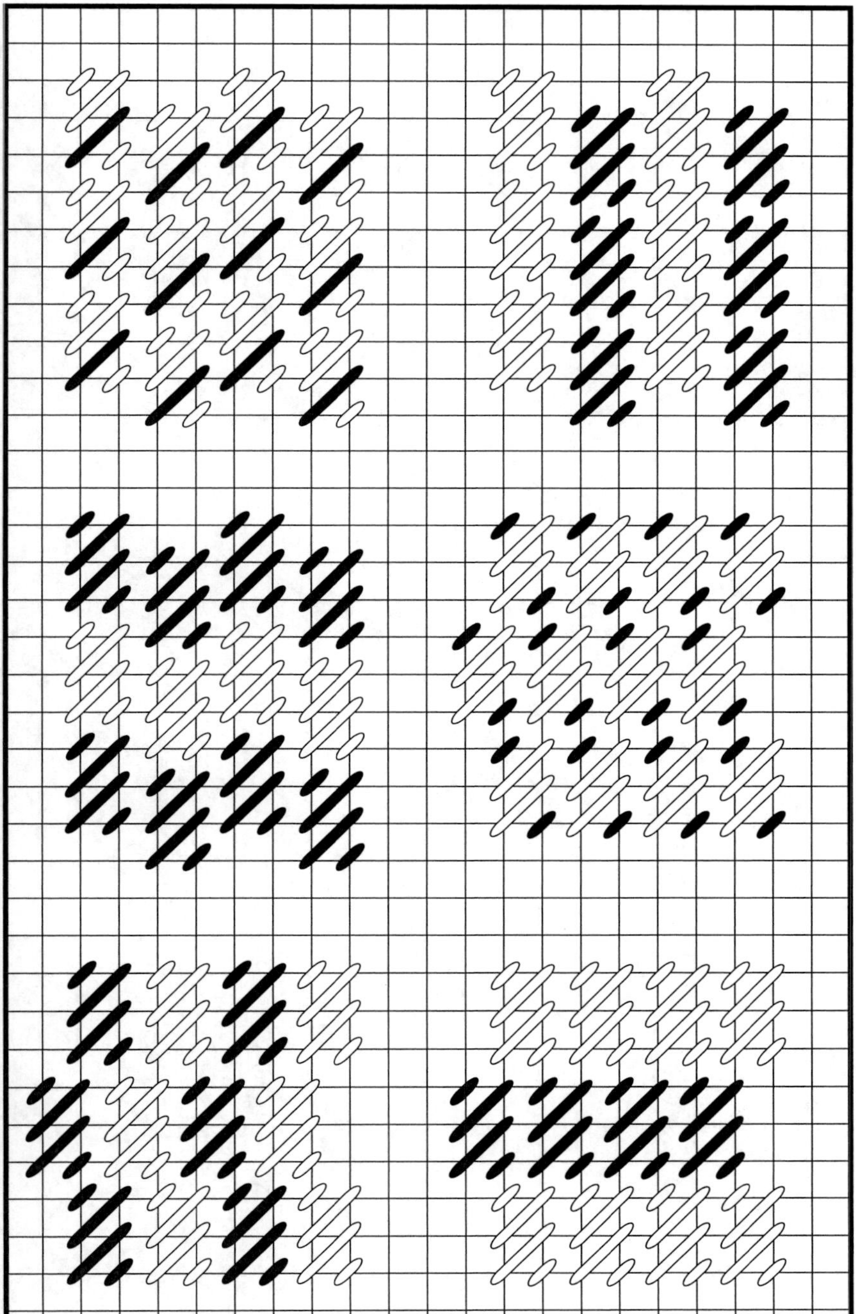

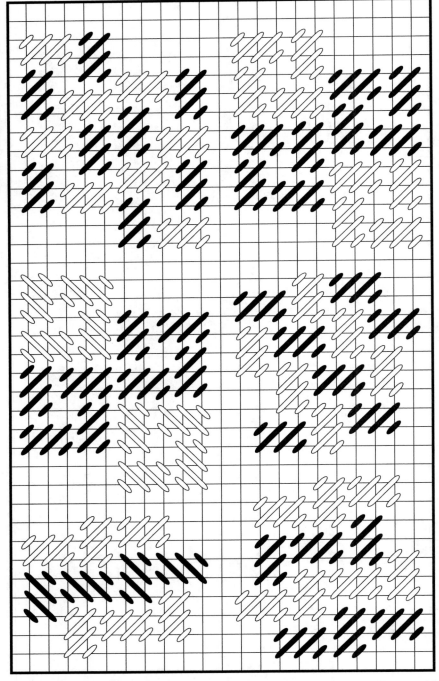

Diagonal Cashmere Stitch

8 6
9 7 4
5 2
3 1

Diagonal Cashmere Stitches

Scotch Stitch

Scotch Stitches

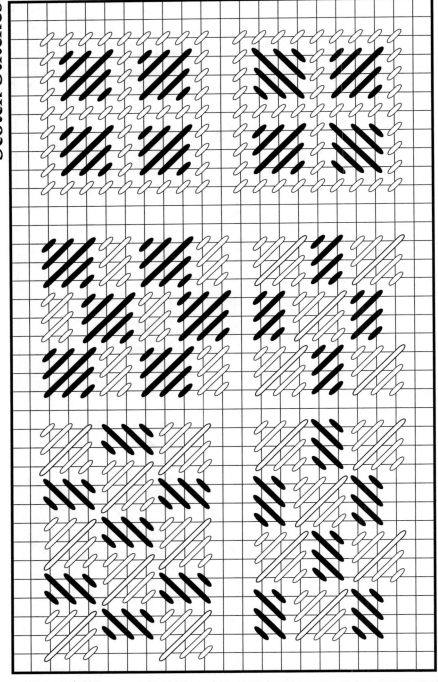

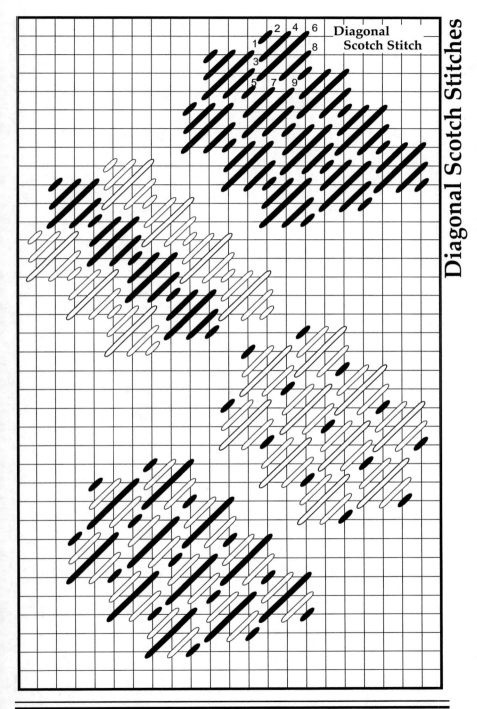

Diagonal Scotch Stitch

2 4 6
1 8
3
5 7 9

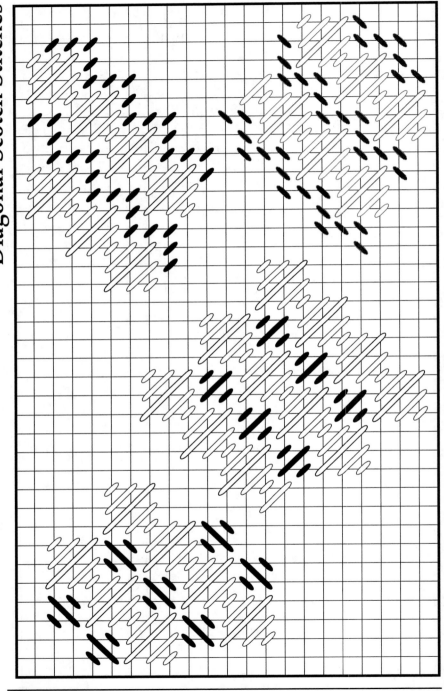

Byzantine Stitch

Byzantine Stitches

Byzantine Stitches

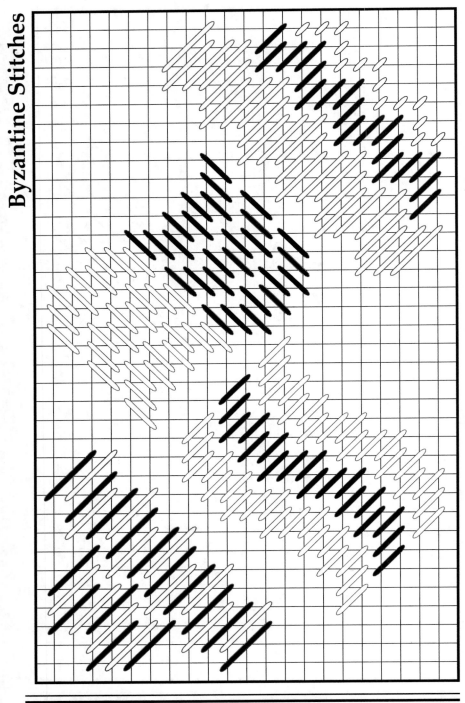

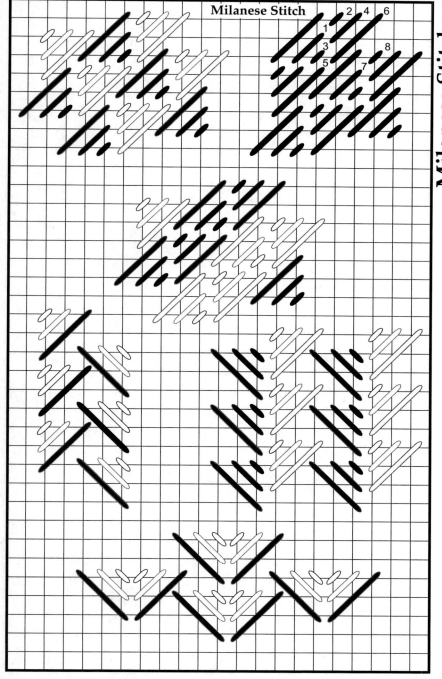

Milanese Stitch

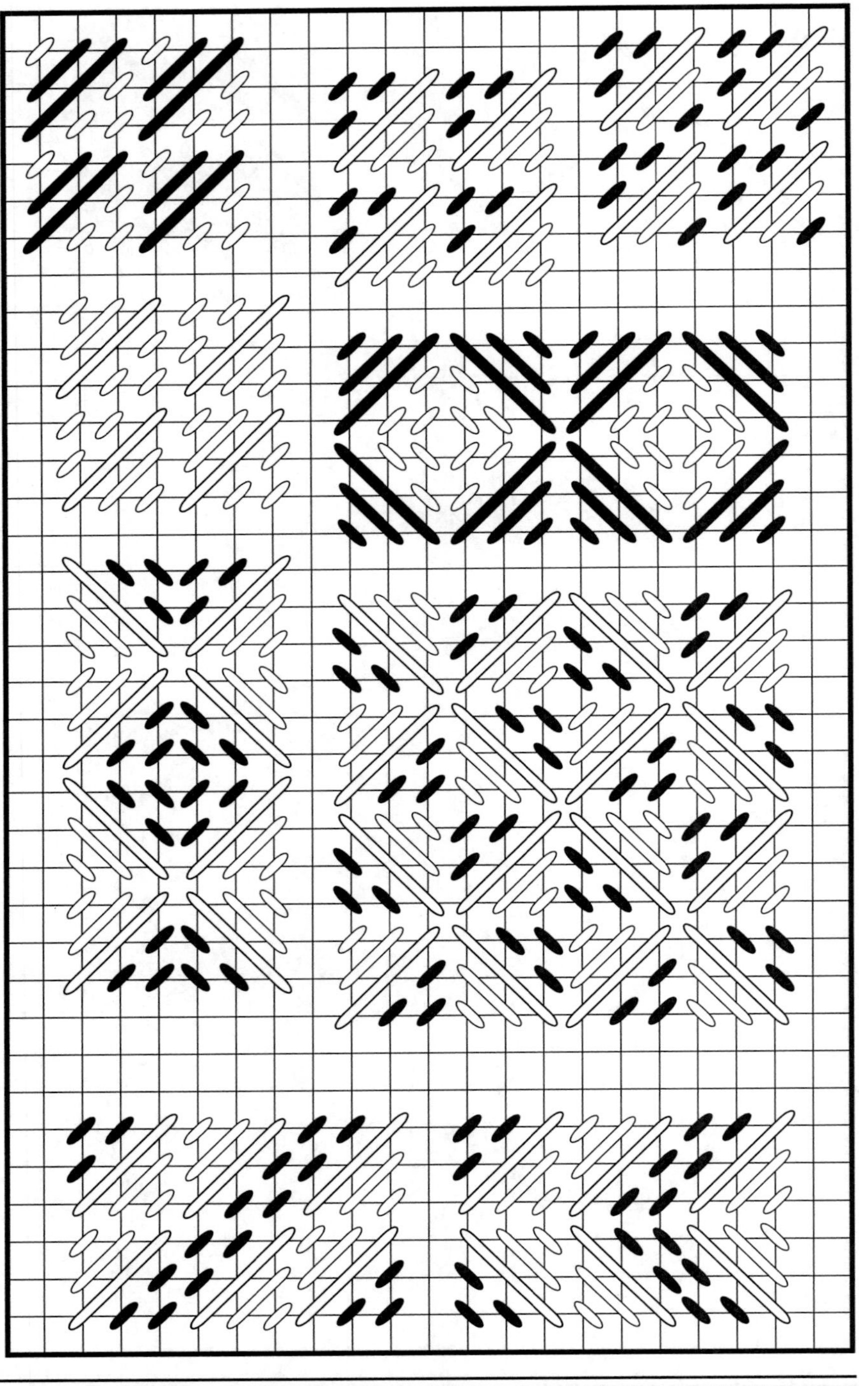

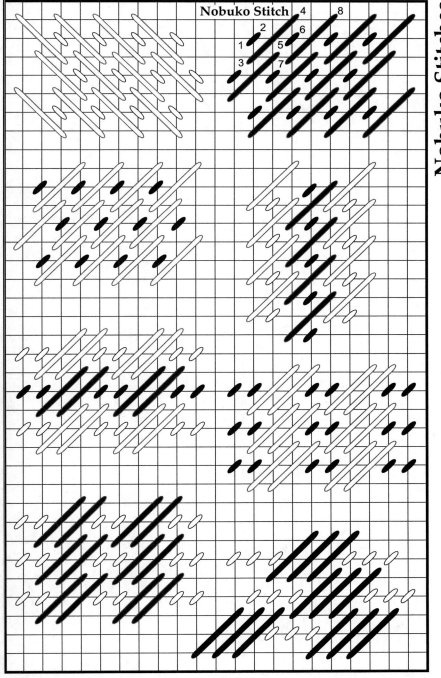

Nobuko Stitch

1 2 3 4 5 6 7 8

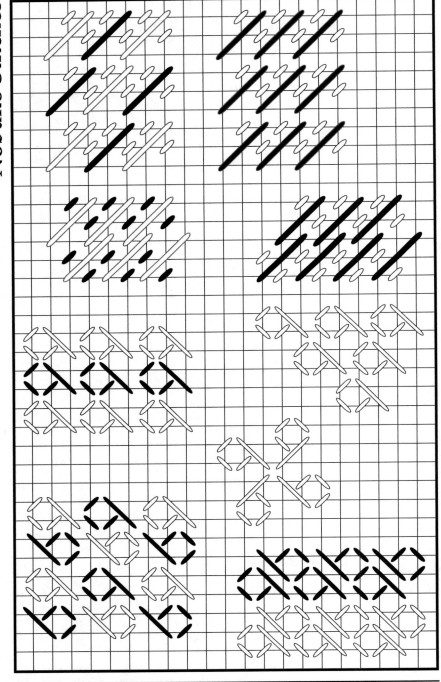

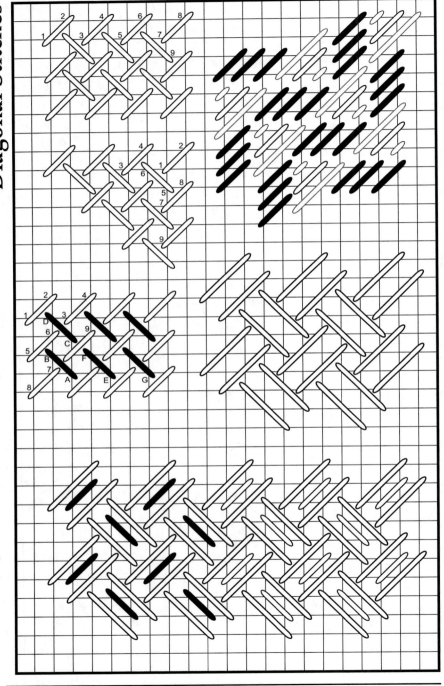

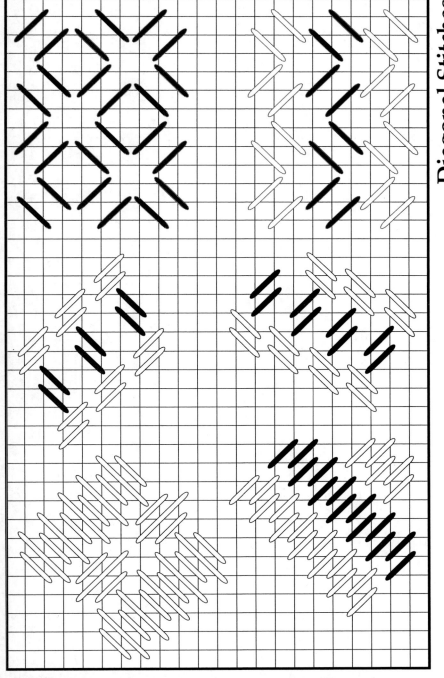

An oblique stitch is one that is neither parallel nor at a right angle to the threads of the canvas. A true diagonal stitch, such as those in the previous section, is oriented on the canvas at a 45° angle. An oblique stitch is slanted at any other angle and can slope in either direction.

Oblique stitches are particularly useful in needlepoint because not only do they cover well, they can take on the direction of the area you are stitching. You get a sense of movement with these patterns, even though the stitch is counted. Choose the slope of the oblique stitch based on the shape of the space you are stitching. Remember that you can even adjust the slope of the pattern within the space as the slope of the space changes.

You can also combine oblique stitches with diagonal or straight stitches to create a unique look. Even if you use the same thread, the change in the angle of the stitch will create a variance in the reflectivity of the light. Remember that you can change the direction of oblique stitches by rotating them. We have shown a number of possibilities, and you can rotate the book to see other variations. Most oblique stitches have four options, holding the book with the top N, S, E and W.

Compensating oblique stitches can sometimes be challenging, because you may have to slightly change the slope of the stitch. Remember that less is more in situations like this; don't try to crowd too many stitches into small spaces.

Oblique Stitches

How Do I Decide What Size Needle to Use?

We feel that this is a matter of personal preference. The thread should go through the eye of the needle easily, and then the needle should go through the canvas without widening the hole. Don't park your needles in the canvas; use magnets for this. If you don't get back to your project right away, an improperly parked needle could damage the canvas.

Should I Use Stretcher Bars?

Always! Even on the smallest canvas! It will make a huge difference in the quality of your work. We use and recommend Evertite™ bars, but if you keep your canvas taut, regular bars will work fine. Attach the canvas with rust-proof tacks or staples. Always tighten the canvas to "Marine standard." You should be able to bounce a quarter off of it! If the canvas can move at all, your carefully laid stitches will be distorted when your piece is framed or otherwise finished. A scroll frame is acceptable for very large canvases, but keep the canvas taut!

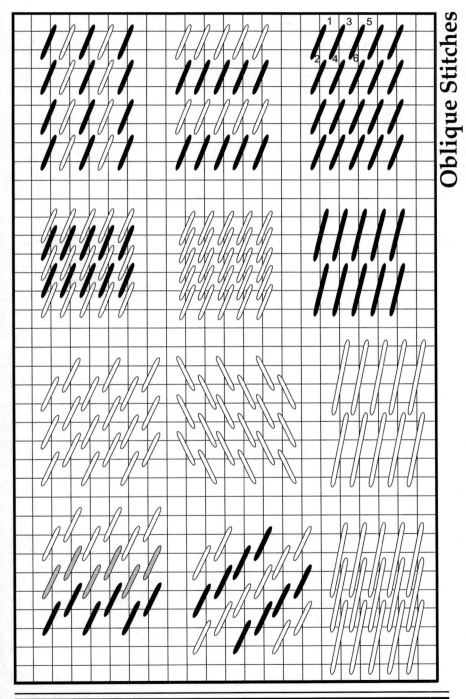

Oblique Stitches

Oblique Stitches

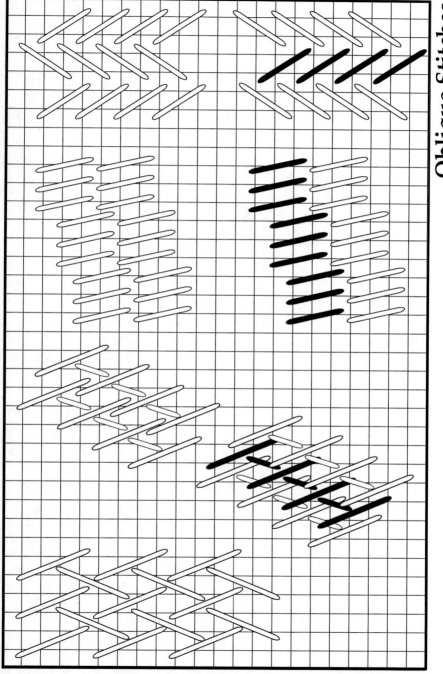

Knitting Stitch

Knitting Stitches

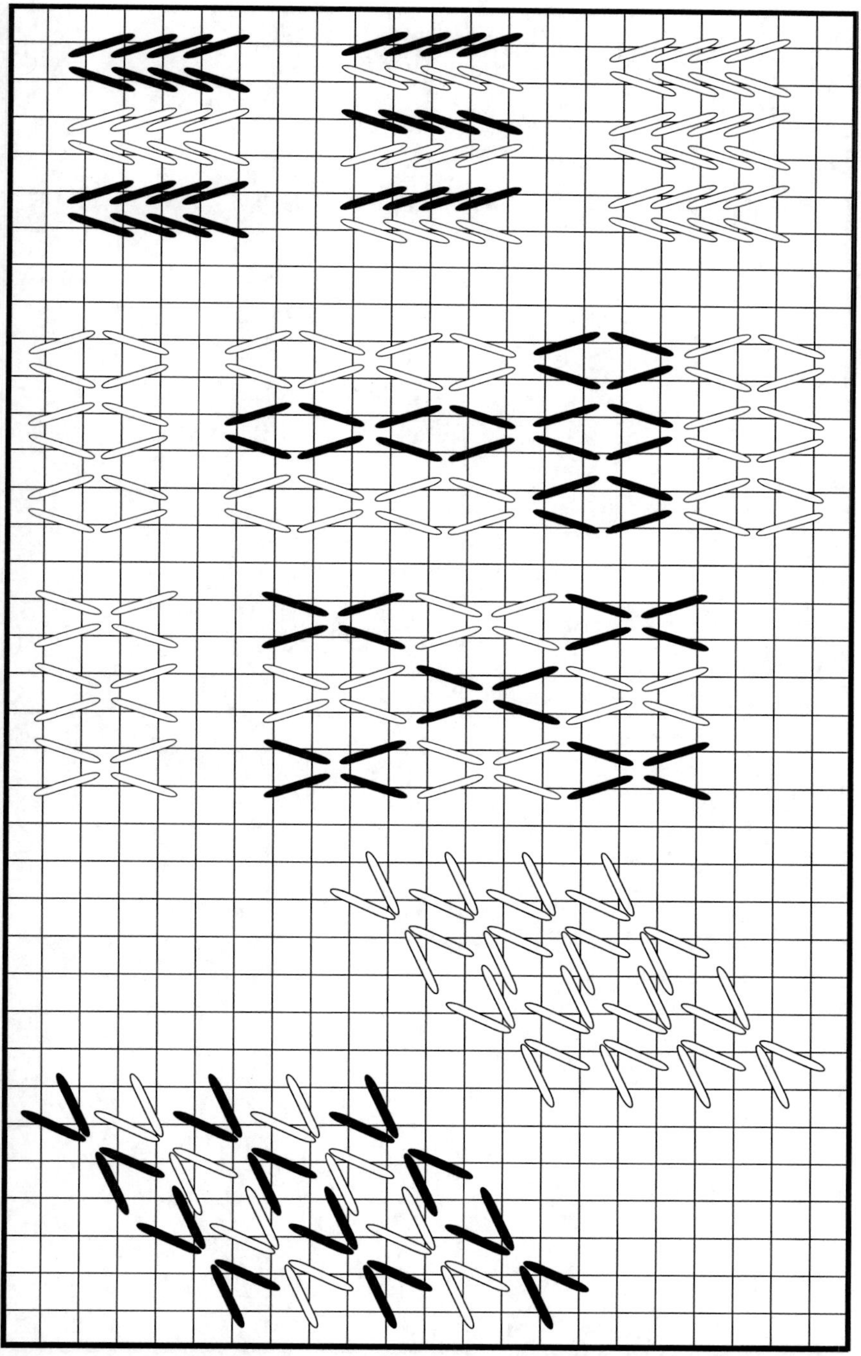

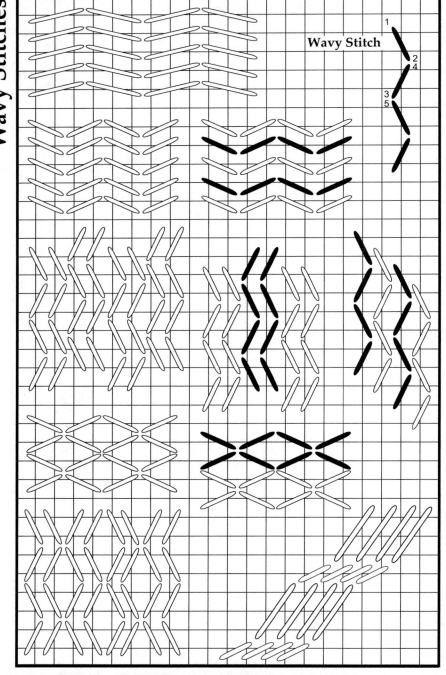

Wavy Stitch

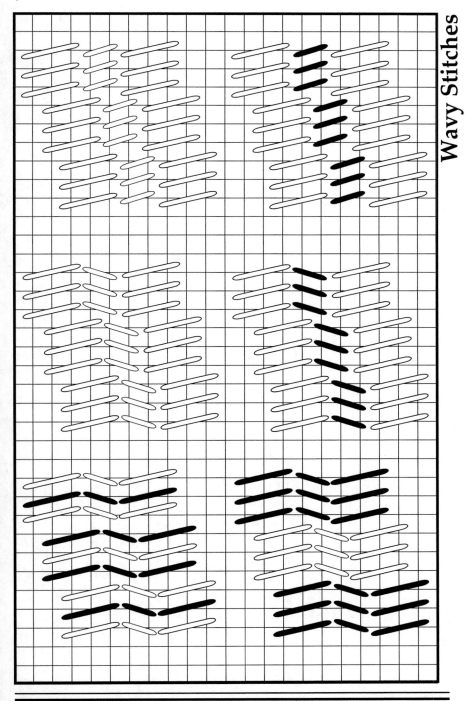

Straight stitches are those that are parallel to the warp or weft threads of the canvas. Any straight stitch can be stitched vertically or horizontally. Use them to form lines or to fill shapes. Many times, a straight stitch is used to make a smooth pattern. It can be any length starting at over one thread to over many threads. Here we are looking at straight stitches for small spaces, so our suggestions are all over 4 canvas threads or less. You can stitch a small space all in one thread and color, or you can vary one or the other, or both. Straight stitches work particularly well for shading in small spaces.

The main difficulty with straight stitches is that they tend not to cover the canvas as well as some of the other types of stitches. It is important to gauge the size of the thread you are using, so that it is neither too thin nor too thick for the area available. If it is too thin, you will be able to see the canvas threads underneath. While this may be a really nice effect on a painted canvas when you plan for it, you don't want it to look like a mistake. If the thread is too thick, it will look crowded and the stitches may not lay straight. Try to find threads that slide smoothly through the canvas, so that they aren't scrunched as they pass through. The smallest stitches (over one thread) may need to be stitched twice (one stitch on top of the other) to make them look as fluffy as the longer stitches.

Compensating straight stitches is easy next to other straight stitches, but annoying next to diagonal stitches. Sometimes it helps to put a row of tent stitches or an outline stitch between the two spaces. Always work straight stitches moving away from you. In other words, come up close to your body and stitch toward the other edge of your canvas.

Stripping, Stroking and Laying Threads

The most important thing you can do to improve your needlepoint is to lay your threads using a laying tool, which can be something as simple as a large needle or as ornate as a glass or wooden handmade tool.

Whenever you stitch with more than a single ply or strand of a thread, or when you are using a ribbon thread, you must lay your stitches carefully. The reason we lay threads is that when threads are laying flat and smooth on the surface of the canvas, they will give the maximum amount of refraction from light. Conversely, if you do not lay such threads, they will resort to their natural tendency to twist, and this is visually jarring and you do not get the proper play of light off the threads.

Laying threads is really a 3-step process consisting of stripping, stroking and laying.
1. *Strip* your thread. Take out the individual plies from the whole strand, and put them back together for stitching.
2. *Stroke* your thread. Before you can lay a stitch on the canvas, you need to stroke the thread with your laying tool in preparation for laying the stitch on the canvas. Make all of the plies or strands of the thread lay parallel to each other before you take the stitch.
3. *Lay* your thread on the canvas. Use the laying tool to control the thread as you place the stitch on the canvas. Slide the tip of your tool out from under the thread at the very last moment before the stitch is completed. Be sure to keep the tip of the tool on top of the stitch until you have the tension of the thread back in your stitching hand, so that your carefully laid stitches do not drift on the canvas.

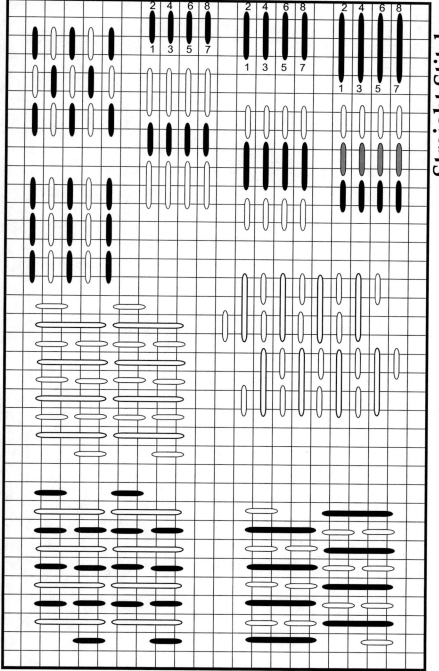

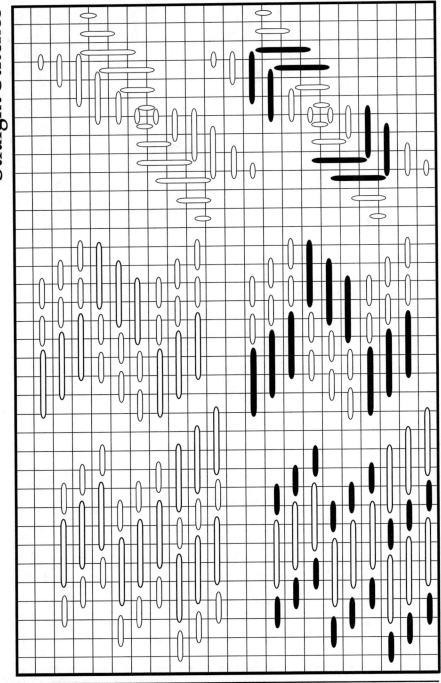

Straight Stitches

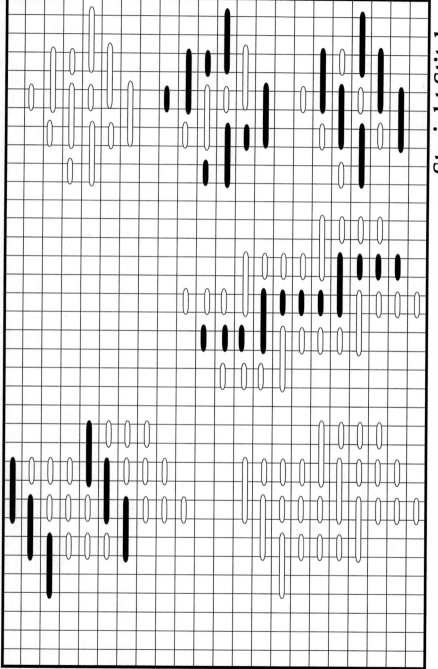

Straight Stitches

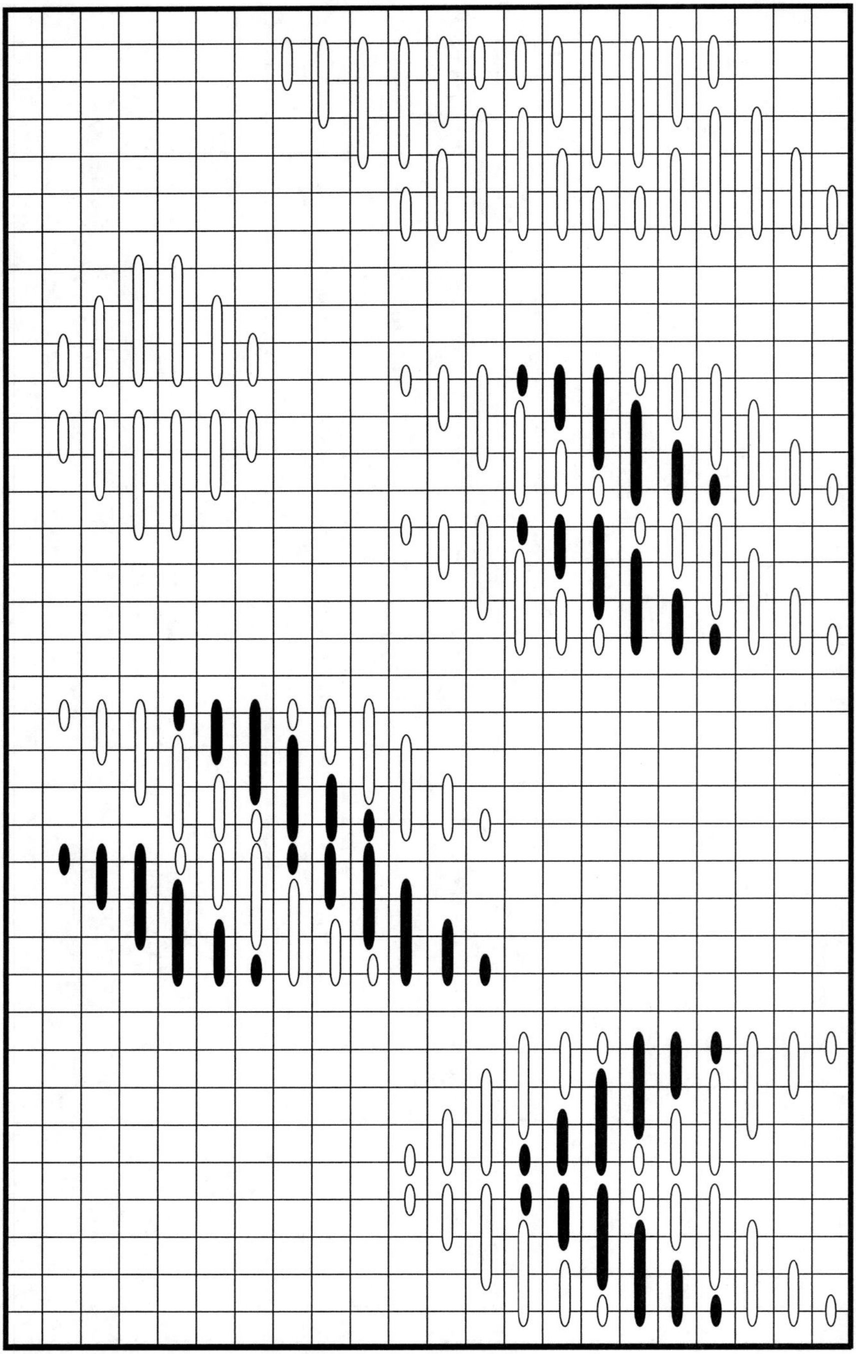

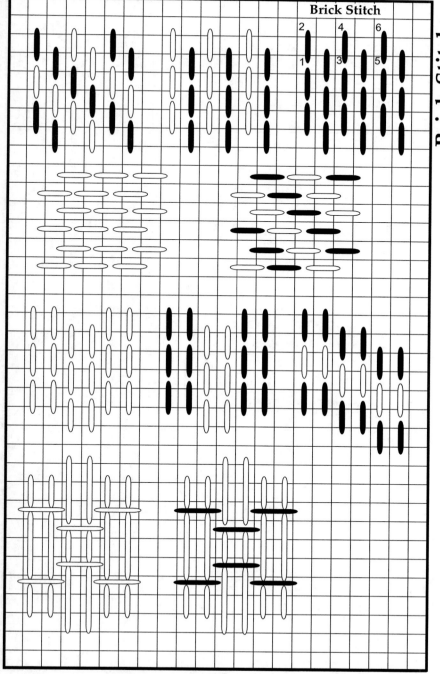

Brick Stitch

2   4   6

1   3   5

Brick Stitches

Brick Stitches

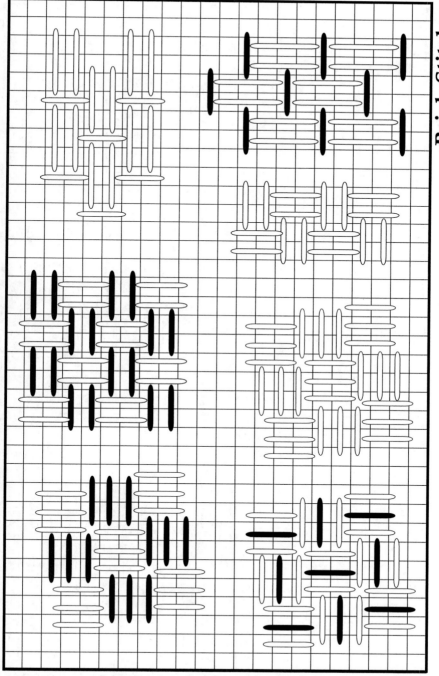

Hungarian Stitches

Hungarian Stitch

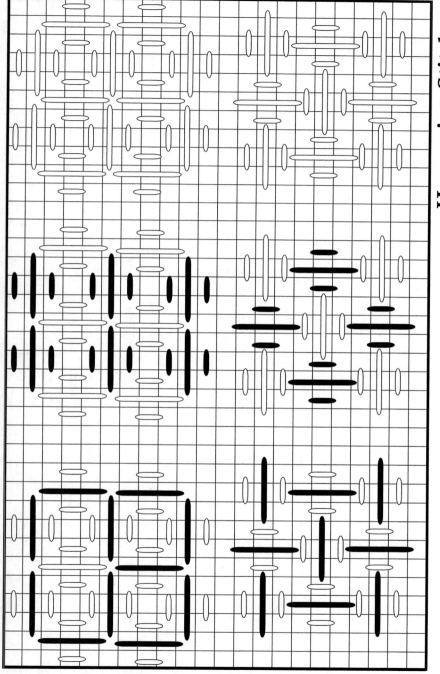

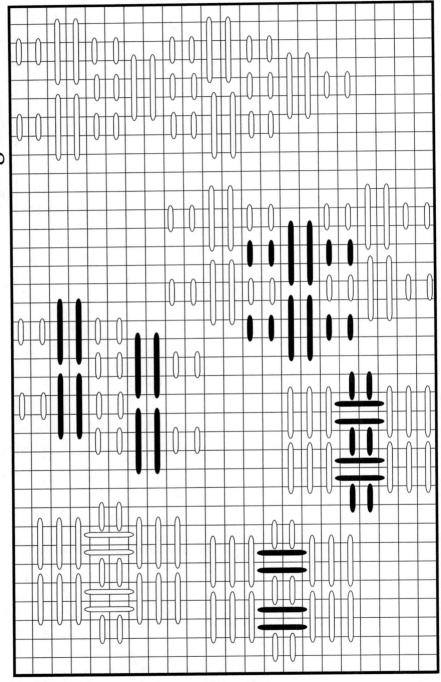

Hungarian Stitches

Cross stitches in needlepoint include a number of related stitches in which the thread is stitched in an 'x' or '+' shape, or combinations of the two. The stitches that make up the cross may be diagonal, oblique or straight. There may be as few as two stitches in the cross, depending on the size of the space and the style of the cross. More complex cross stitches may be composed of many stitches.

Cross stitches are excellent for needlepoint because they cover well, compensate well, and are easily manipulated. They work well in both solid and multi-color threads, and in combinations of threads. You can create different textures by changing the top stitch of the cross. You can fill an odd-shaped tiny space by adjusting the length of the legs of a single multiple cross stitch.

Our favorite stitch for outlines and letters is a cross stitch over one intersection, because you don't get the jagged effect that can be a problem with a tent stitch outline. Slightly larger cross stitches make a nice texture, particularly in silk. Combinations of cross stitches with diagonal, oblique, and straight stitches can be very effective, but be careful in smaller spaces not to use too many different elements.

In needlepoint, you should cross each cross stitch unit as you go. If you come from a counted-thread background, you may have been told to work the bottom stitch across an area, and then to come back with the top stitches, but on canvas (and particularly with multi-colored threads), it is preferable to complete each unit before you go on to the next one.

Fibers and Threads

Fibers are materials that come from animals or plants, or are man-made. This could be linen, wool, silk, cotton, rayon or bamboo! *Threads* are made from those fibers using a variety of methods such as spinning, twisting, or chaining. We do not stitch with plain fibers; we stitch with threads that are made from those fibers. You do not shop for fibers for your painted canvas; you shop for threads.

Do I Start By Choosing Threads or Stitches?

There's no one answer to that question. If you want to pick a stitch for an area, you should consider what thread you are using, and vice versa. We suggest pulling out a pile of threads for your canvas in colors you like. Pick threads with which you love to stitch. If you hate rayon, don't consider rayon threads. If you love cotton, pick lots of threads made from cotton. Choose thin threads and thick threads, threads that need to be laid, and threads that do not, but most of all, pick threads that you love to stroke! It's all about texture.

Now, consider a single area: what threads might work here? Choose a few stitches. Which thread will work with which stitch? Do you want canvas to show or do you need to cover a color you don't like?

The bottom line is that stitches and threads work together - you can't pick one without the other!

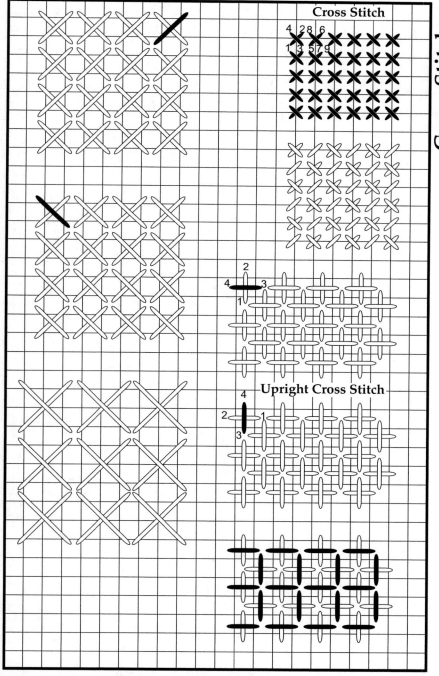

Cross Stitch

4 | 2 8 | 6
1 | 3 5 | 7 9

Upright Cross Stitch

2
4 — 3
1

4
2 — 1
3

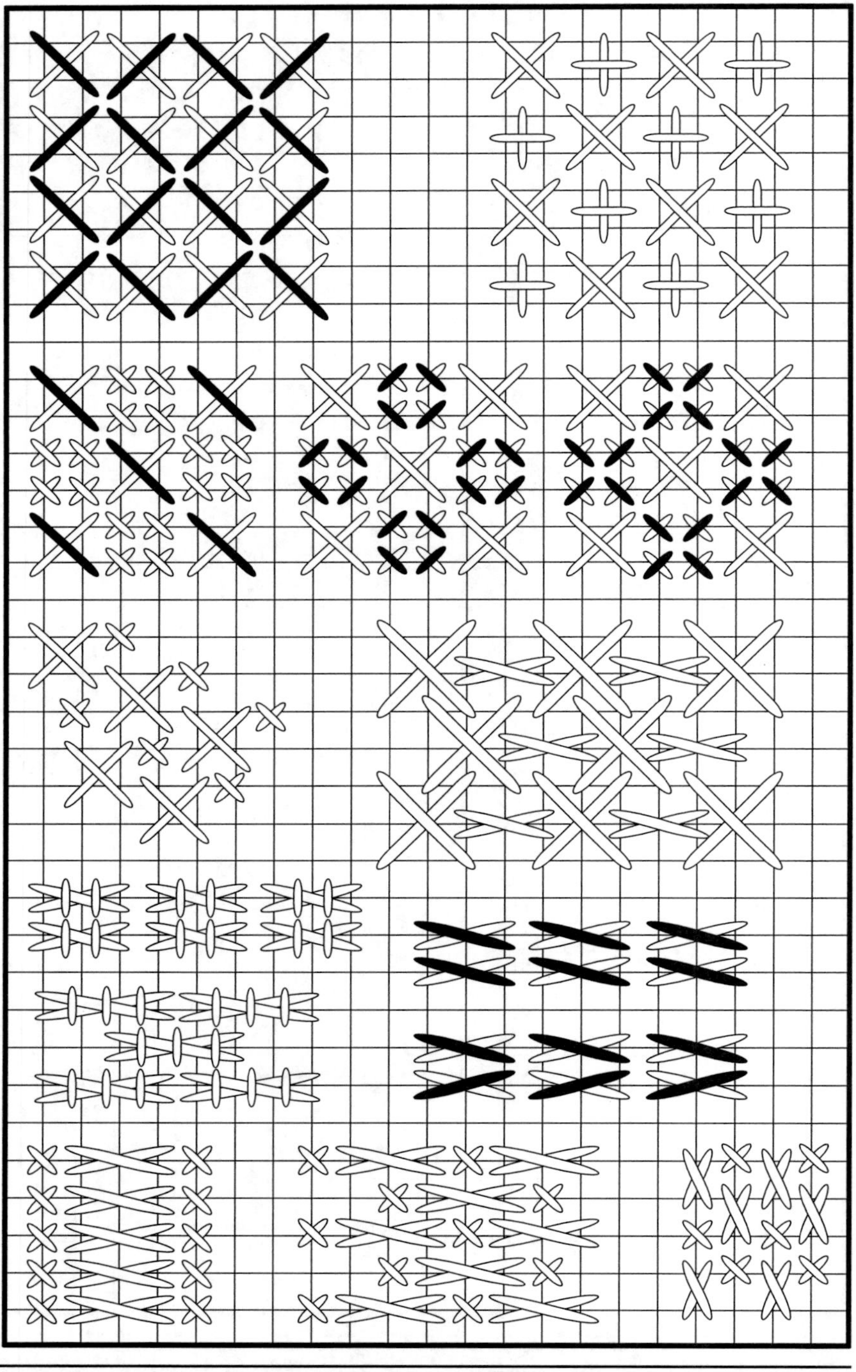

Smyrna Cross Stitches

Layered Cross Stitches

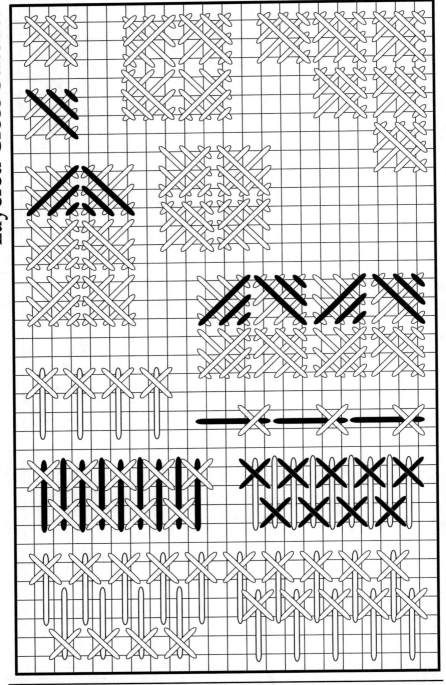

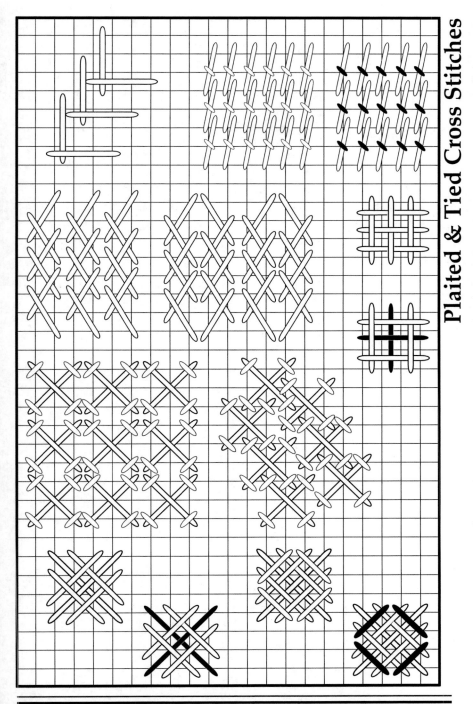

Plaited & Tied Cross Stitches

Plaited & Tied Cross Stitches

Plaited & Tied Cross Stitches

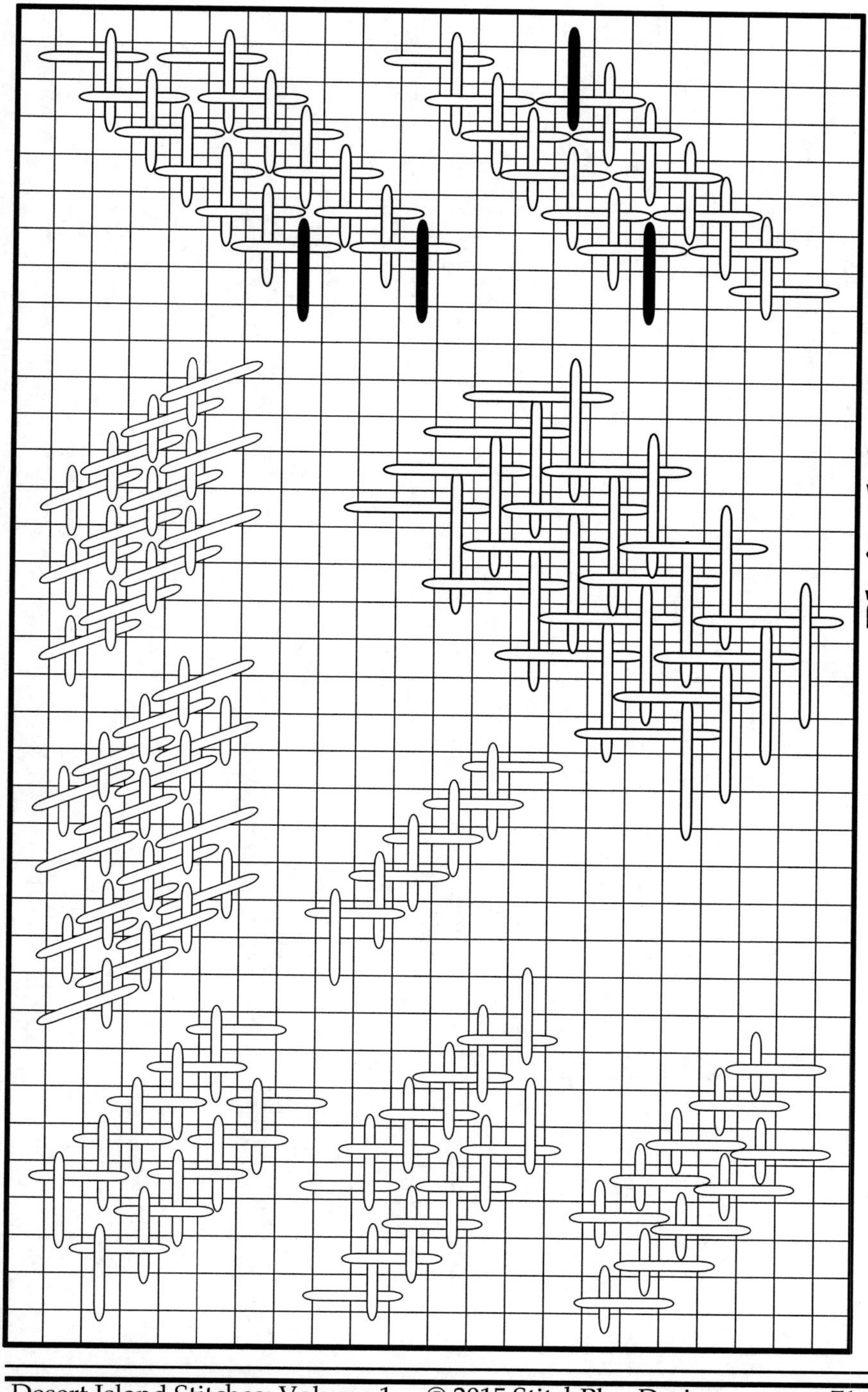

Plaited & Tied Cross Stitches

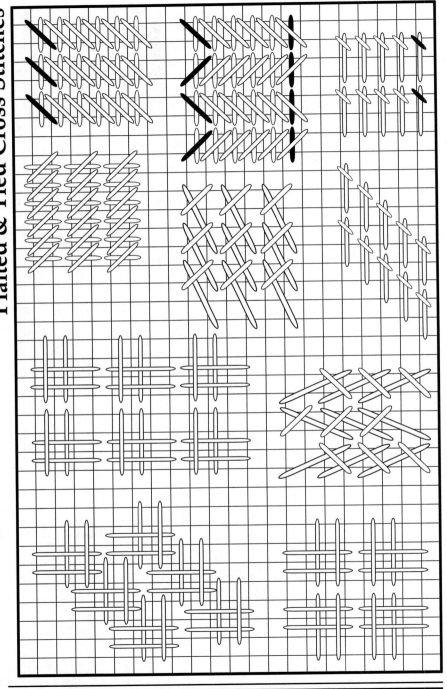

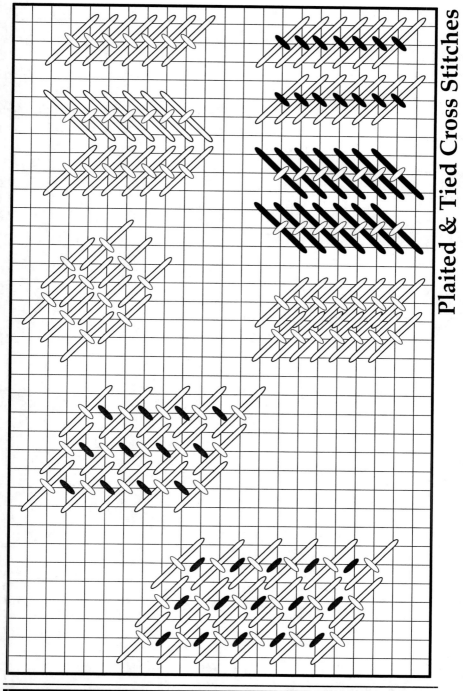

Plaited & Tied Cross Stitches

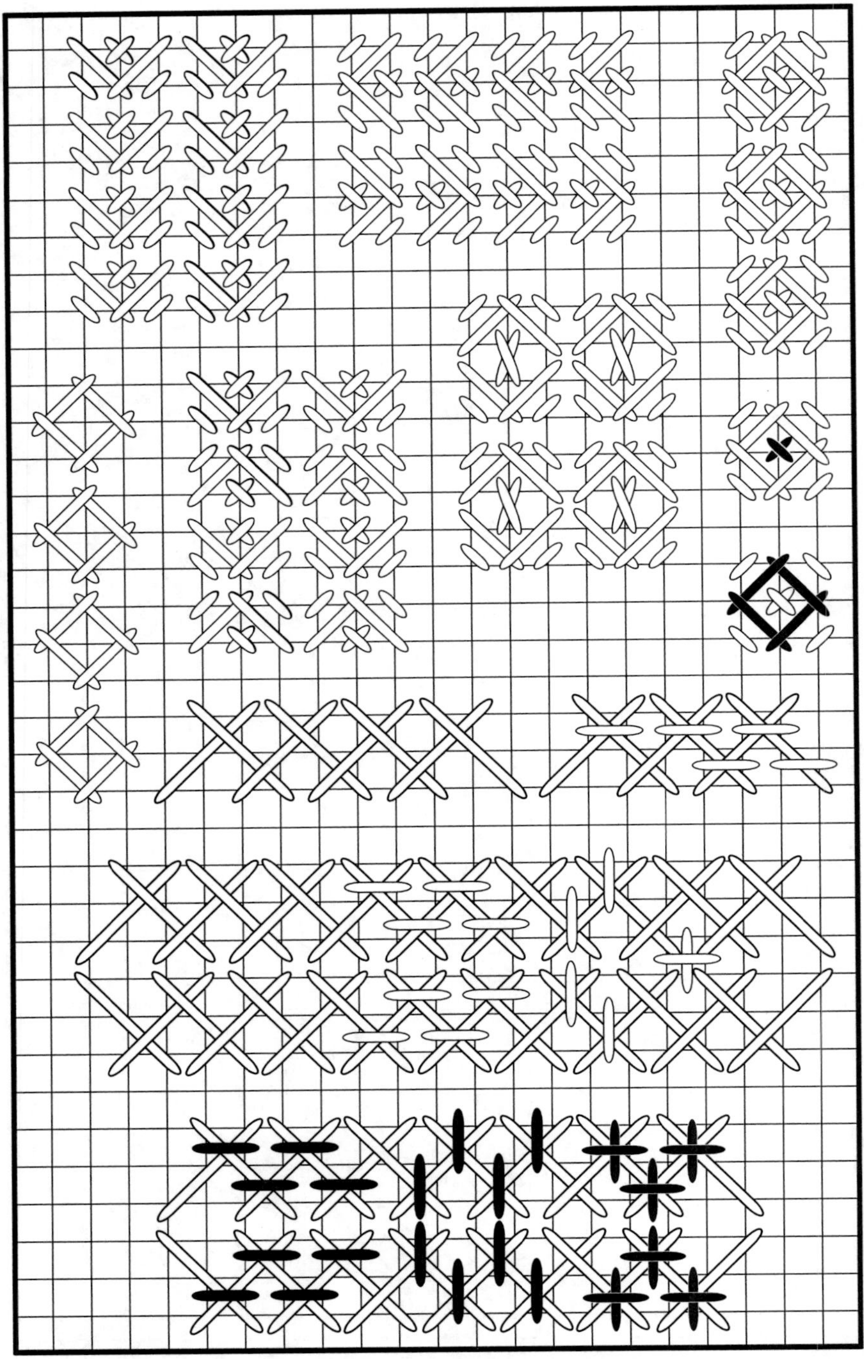

Plaited & Tied Cross Stitches

Multiple Cross Stitches

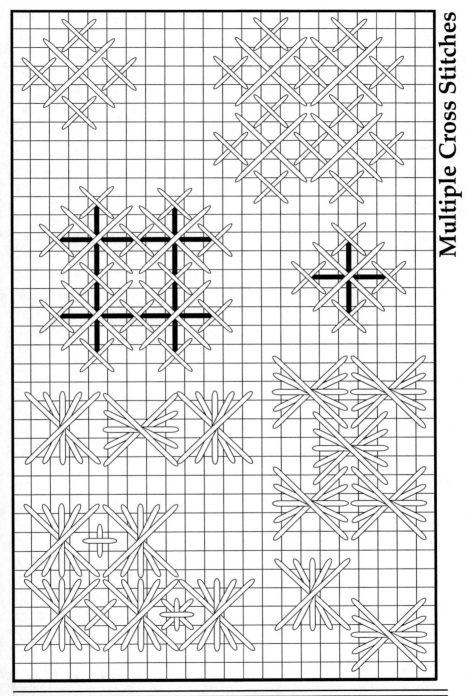

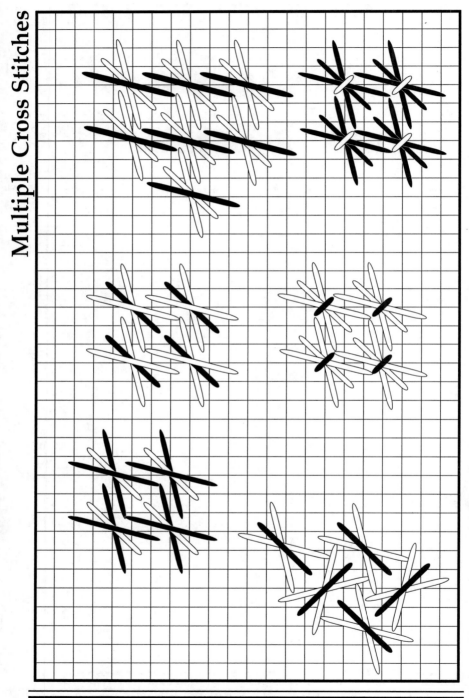